Gardênia Conceição Santos de Souza
Eliana Lessa Cordeiro
Liniker Scolfild Rodrigues da Silva

# Cognitive Decline: Knowing the Elderly and Understanding their Caregiver

Gardênia Conceição Santos de Souza
Eliana Lessa Cordeiro
Liniker Scolfild Rodrigues da Silva

# Cognitive Decline: Knowing the Elderly and Understanding their Caregiver

## Caring and being cared for

ScienciaScripts

**Imprint**
Any brand names and product names mentioned in this book are subject to trademark, brand or patent protection and are trademarks or registered trademarks of their respective holders. The use of brand names, product names, common names, trade names, product descriptions etc. even without a particular marking in this work is in no way to be construed to mean that such names may be regarded as unrestricted in respect of trademark and brand protection legislation and could thus be used by anyone.

Cover image: www.ingimage.com

This book is a translation from the original published under ISBN 978-613-9-62117-0.

Publisher:
Sciencia Scripts
is a trademark of
Dodo Books Indian Ocean Ltd. and OmniScriptum S.R.L publishing group

120 High Road, East Finchley, London, N2 9ED, United Kingdom
Str. Armeneasca 28/1, office 1, Chisinau MD-2012, Republic of Moldova, Europe
Printed at: see last page
ISBN: 978-620-7-71343-1

# CONTENTS

# PREFACE

Various areas of the health field arouse diverse interests, and seeking knowledge is something that makes someone different. This book comes with a bold proposal to bring together studies in a unique way, showing through very specific research topics such as: Profile of the Elderly and Analysis of the Domains of a Depressive Symptom Scale; Profile of Caregivers of the Elderly and Analysis of the Domains of an Overload Scale; and Sociodemographic Profile of the Elderly in a Health District.

The field of health is permeated by constantly changing information. Differentiated research, with extensive knowledge and quality about something or someone becomes a valuable way of understanding and drawing up a specific profile with conclusive and meaningful data. Given this scenario, the studies that will be covered in this book provide a reflection on varied groups, which can be studied and used as bridges for new research and studies.

The first chapter of the book deals with a quantitative study, which aims to identify the sociodemographic profile of caregivers of the elderly and analyze their responses to the domains of a depression scale, allowing the collection of data and a broader view of the issues related to symptoms of depression. The second chapter deals with the profile of caregivers of the elderly and the consequences that overload can have on their lives and their interpersonal relationships, while the third chapter focuses on the profile of the elderly. All the studies were designed to integrate each other. The research that makes up this book was carried out in Health District IV, in the municipality of Recife, capital of the state of Pernambuco - Brazil, and it was in the interest of bringing together as much information as possible on the subject of public health issues with a focus on gerontology. This is a book of great relevance to the study and knowledge of the work of professionals in the field of preventive health.

In view of the above, this issue aims to contribute to scientific knowledge. The aim is to favor and raise results for new studies in the field of Gerontology. We dedicate this book to all readers who are eager to seek out new knowledge. Finally, we would like to express our gratitude to those who recognize this work and the dedication that went into writing it.

# CHAPTER 01: PROFILE OF CARERS OF THE ELDERLY AND ANALYSIS OF THE DOMAINS OF A DEPRESSIVE SYMPTOM SCALE


[1]Gardênia Conceiçâo Santos de Souza,[2] Eliana Lessa Cordeiro,[3] Liniker Scolfild Rodrigues da Silva,[4] Fernanda Santos Cavalcanti,[4] Izis Santana da Silva,[4] Karla Roberta Leite de Lima,[4] Dayse Andrielle Viana da Silva,[4] Maria Jocélia Silva de Souza,[4] Luana Carla de Andrade Palha,[4] Diana Marques Cunha,[4] Carlos Henrique da Silva Ferreira.

[1]Master's Degree in Gerontology from the Federal University of Pernambuco (UFPE). Recife

(PE), Brazil. E-mail: gardeniacss@yahoo.com.br

[2]Master's degree in Neuropsychiatry and Behavioral Sciences from the

Federal University of

Pernambuco (UFPE). Recife (PE), Brazil. E-mail:

elianalessa18@hotmail.com

[3]Resident in the Multiprofessional Residency Program in Collective Health at the Faculty of Medical Sciences (FCM) and the University of Pernambuco (UPE).

Recife, Pernambuco (PE), Brazil. E-mail: liniker_14@hotmail.com

[4]Nurses (graduates), Salgado de Oliveira University (UNIVERSO). Recife, Pernambuco (PE), Brazil. E-mail: fernandacsantos.87@gmail.com;

izisantana@,gmail.com; karlaroberta571_@gmail.com; andrielledaysev@gmail.com; joocelia@gmail.com; luanapalha@gmail.com; diana.marques.cunha@gmail.com;

carlos.henrique.sf.ch@gmail.com


---


## SUMMARY

**Objective:** **To** identify the sociodemographic profile of elderly caregivers and to evaluate their response to the domains and items of a depression scale. **Method:** This is a cross-sectional study with a quantitative approach, in which the CES-D scale was used to analyze the domains and their items, with a sample of 228 questionnaires, applied to caregivers of elderly people registered with the Family Health Program of Health District IV, with the inclusion criterion being age over 28 and at least 10 years of living with the elderly. **Results:** The study showed that the profile of caregivers of the elderly is predominantly female, aged between 50 and 60, with primary schooling, married or in a stable union and with social class D-E. As for the analysis of the scale's domains and items, there was a prevalence of the answer "rarely" for the mood, somatic symptoms, interpersonal relationship and "not being able to get on with my things" domains, showing that in this population these domains and items mostly functioned as protective effects for depression. As for the positive effects, two items proved to be protective, with one item signaling a negative effect. **Conclusion:** This study showed the importance of using the CES-D scale and the analysis of the domains and items to screen for depressive symptoms in caregivers of the elderly and that this reading, depending on the response, can indicate protective factors for depression, which becomes richer when complemented with the profile of these caregivers.

**Keywords:** Depression; Caregivers; Elderly.

## INTRODUCTION

Brazil is going through a period of demographic change, as the decline in mortality and fertility and the growth of health care technologies have increased life expectancy, thus generating an increase in the ageing population. This has led to a transformation in the epidemiological profile of the population, with an increase in chronic diseases, which can compromise the autonomy of the elderly, causing them to need permanent care from their family and/or caregiver (AGUIAR et al, 2011).

The caregiver is the person responsible for assisting the sick or dependent person, facilitating their day-to-day activities, such as feeding and personal hygiene, as well as administering routine medication and accompanying them to health services, excluding tasks or procedures identified as exclusive to other legally established professions (GRATÂO et al, 2012).

There are two types of caregivers: formal caregivers, who are generally employed by the family to carry out care activities, in which case they have an employment relationship, and informal caregivers, who are members of the elderly person's family or related to them, such as friends, neighbors, church members, support groups, among others, and thus take on care and assistance activities (PEREIRA et al, 2013).

This experience of taking on the care of the elderly can often cause stress and exhaustion, in which the caregiver, when carrying out activities related to the physical and psychosocial well-being of the elderly, starts to have restrictions on their own life, exposing themselves to stressful situations, such as the burden of basic tasks, the illnesses that arise and the priority needs. Allied to these factors, there are also other problems, such as a lack of information, physical, psychological and financial support to cope with the daily routine of caring (STACKFLETH et al, 2012).

Therefore, in many cases, they can lead these caregivers to develop a process of depression, characterized by an immense and lasting change in the individual's state of mind, in addition to showing a loss of energy and interest, a sense of guilt, changes in social behavior, difficulty concentrating, lack of appetite and thoughts of death (OLIVEIRA, 2012).

The purpose of this article was to identify the sociodemographic profile of caregivers of the elderly and to analyze their responses to the domains of a depression scale. The sample was also characterized in terms of age, gender, schooling, marital status and social class, as well as listing the domains of the CES-D scale and condensing them into specific tables for each one.

## METHOD

This is a cross-sectional descriptive quantitative study which aims to identify the sociodemographic profile of caregivers of the elderly and analyze their responses to the domains of a depression scale. It was carried out in the Family Health Programs (PSF's) of District IV of the city of Recife/PE, considering as a reference a significant demand for care for the elderly and their caregivers.

A total of 228 people over the age of 28 were interviewed who reported on the cognitive status of the elderly and who had lived with them for more than 10 years, providing help and care for them. The research data was collected by applying a structured questionnaire with closed questions that addressed the research problem.

For data collection, we used the CES-D (CENTRE FOR EPIDEMIOLOGIC STUDIES OF DEPRESSION) survey instrument, translated and semantically validated for Brazil by Silveira & Jorge in a study of adolescents and by Tavares (2004) who studied the psychometric characteristics of the CES-D in relation to the GDS (*Geriatric Depression Scale*) in the elderly. The questionnaire has four domains with 20 items and a cut-off point of 16 and allows for an assessment of the frequency of depressive symptoms experienced in the week prior to the interview. Each item allows four answers (never or rarely, for a short time, for a moderate time, and for most of the time), which include questions relating to the following domains: mood, somatic symptoms, social interactions and positive affect (BATISTONI et al, 2010).

This survey was complemented by a sociodemographic questionnaire, which used the Brazilian economic classification criteria (ABEP/2014) as its theoretical premise. It was applied to caregivers of the elderly in district IV and its results were presented with the aim of identifying the profile of this sample.

The questionnaire and the Informed Consent Form (ICF) were applied individually and, once answered, sealed in individual envelopes used for manual compilation and for creating graphs and tables in the Excel 2010 program. The results were presented as absolute and relative frequencies. The sociodemographic questionnaire was used to ascertain the profile of elderly caregivers.

The study complied with Resolution 466/12 of the National Health Council (CNS), which is based on the ethical and legal principles that emanate from statements and guidelines on research involving human beings, and was approved by the Research Ethics Committee (CEP) of the Federal University of Pernambuco (UFPE) under CAAE: 48403115.8.0000.5208. It is worth noting that this article is part of the master's thesis of the supervisor professor Gardênia Conceiçâo Santos de Souza and the PIC (Scientific Initiation Program) of the Salgado de Oliveira University (UNIVERSO), Recife-PE Campus, of which the authors are members.

## RESULTS AND DISCUSSION

The description in table 01 shows the social characterization of the informants of elderly people in district IV, carried out in Recife between October 2015 and April 2016. Among the sociodemographic variables of the caregivers, the following predominated: female gender (81.58%), age 50 to 60 (25.88%), elementary school education (43%), and married or in a stable union (42.10%).

**Table 01. Social characterization of the elderly informant in Health District IV. Recife, October/2015 to April/2016.**

| Variables | n = 228 | % |
| --- | --- | --- |
| sex | | |

| Female | 186 | 81,58 |
|---|---|---|
| Male | 42 | 18,42 |
| **Age** | | |
| 28 --\| 38 | 49 | 21,5 |
| 39 --\| 49 | 47 | 20,61 |
| 50 --\| 60 | 59 | 25,88 |
| 61 --\| 71 | 53 | 23,24 |
| > 72. | 20 | 8,77 |
| **Education** | | |
| Illiterate | 25 | 11,0 |
| Fundamental | 98 | 43,0 |
| Medium | 81 | 35,5 |
| Superior | 24 | 10,5 |
| **Marital status** | | |
| Single | 95 | 41,67 |
| Married or in a stable union | 96 | 42,10 |
| Viùvo | 19 | 8,33 |
| Other | 18 | 7,90 |

According to Tomomitsu et al, (2013), in relation to gender attributions, women are more present in the care of the elderly, and most of them are wives or daughters of the elderly.

For women, caregiving consists of various roles in the domestic sphere, passed down from generation to generation and thus becoming something natural. There is a definition of household chores in families that is carried out by members in different situations, so that, in the future, this lived experience can be a determining factor in becoming a caregiver, and this task of caring can also be influenced by social and cultural factors (OLIVEIRA; D'ELBOUX, 2012).

Regarding the average age of caregivers, the highest prevalence was between 50 and 60 years (25.88%), followed by 61 and 71 years (23.24%), with a small difference between these variables. Most caregivers of the elderly are middle-aged, as they are culturally included in Brazilian society, which allows children, husbands and wives to care for the elderly (SANTOS, 2011).

According to Pereira (2012), advanced age can be a worrying factor for caregivers of the elderly, as it can represent physical and functional limits due to the ageing process.

As for the level of education, the majority had primary education, followed by secondary education, with higher education having the lowest level. As such, Oliveira and D'Elboux (2012) state that a low level of education can have a direct and negative impact on the activities of caregivers in understanding the process of the elderly becoming ill, with a drop in the quality of the services provided combined with a lack of information, which can cause great emotional tension and stress for these caregivers.

Therefore, it can be seen that a lack of knowledge can lead to negative care for the elderly, due to the low level of schooling reported in the survey by elderly caregivers.

In many cases, the lack of employment outside the home, due to a low level of education, leads individuals to take on the role of caregiver. Even in the face of all the difficulties, they show satisfaction in this job, since most of the time they are their relatives (YAMASHITA et al, 2013).

With regard to marital status, we found that married or in a stable union predominated over the others. Araùjo et al, (2013) state that this data points to an important item: caring for the elderly combined with marital and household responsibilities. A positive point occurs when the caregiver has the help of their spouse.

In this context, Santos (2013) points out that both situations, married or single, can intervene positively or negatively in care. The married situation, when associated with the spouse, facilitates support for the tasks carried out with the elderly; on the other hand, if this does not happen, it can generate discomfort, because, in addition to caring for the elderly, this caregiver will still be responsible for other household tasks.

Santos (2013) also adds that being single can be a concern when the caregiver allows their care tasks to interfere as a negative influence on their personal life.

**Table 02. Social Class Brazil (ABEP, 2015) of caregivers of the elderly in Health District IV. Recife, October/2015 to April/2016.**

| Variables | Points | n = 228 | % |
|---|---|---|---|
| A | 45-100 | 04 | 02 |
| B1 | 38-44 | 10 | 4.3 |
| B2 | 29-37 | 34 | 15 |
| C1 | 23-28 | 53 | 23.2 |
| C2 | 17-22 | 55 | 24 |
| D-E | 0-16 | 72 | 31.5 |

Table 02 shows the characterization of the social class Brazil (ABEP, 2015) of caregivers of the elderly in district IV in Recife in the period from October 2015 to April 2016, where it can be seen that the majority of informants (31%) belong to social class D-E. Araùjo (2013) states in his study that most caregivers are not financially rewarded because they are family caregivers and, in order to support their family, they have to resort to other means of secondary employment.

Filippin et al, (2014) say that the higher the financial status of their interviewees, the worse their outlook on life, related to a greater demand to always obtain better conditions. Good financial conditions, access to information, culture and knowledge can change the citizen, making them more rigorous about their well-being and, through the depression scales and their domains, depressive symptoms were verified.

**Table 03. Mood domain of the CES-D Scale presented by caregivers of the elderly in Health District IV. Recife, October/2015 to April/2016.**

| During the last week: | Rarely | For a short time | For a moderate amount of time | Most of the time |
|---|---|---|---|---|
| 03. I couldn't improve my mood | 130 | 35 | 30 | 33 |
| 06. I felt depressed | 132 | 30 | 30 | 36 |
| 09. My life was a failure | 164 | 28 | 21 | 15 |
| 10. I felt frightened | 145 | 30 | 31 | 22 |
| 13. Talk less about usual | 133 | 29 | 37 | 29 |
| 14. I felt alone | 136 | 23 | 34 | 35 |

| | | | |
|---|---|---|---|
| **17. I had a crying spell** | 156 | 30 | 17 | 25 |
| **18. I felt sad** | 122 | 33 | 38 | 35 |

Table 03 shows the analysis of the mood domain of the scale, which shows that among all the items (3, 6, 9, 10, 13, 14, 17 and 18) corresponding to: I couldn't improve my mood (57%), I felt depressed (57.9%), my life was a failure (72%), I felt frightened (63.6%), I talked less than usual (58.3%), I felt lonely (60%), I had a crying crisis (68.4%), I felt sad (53.5%), the highest percentage occurred for the answer rarely (less than a day).

The existing challenges, restlessness about the future, exhaustion, stress, discouragement, sadness, worry, lack of time for social and leisure activities provide significant peculiarities for the negative conception of the quality of life of caregivers (FILIPPIN et al, 2014). The study showed that, for this sample, these factors did not influence the onset of depressive symptoms because they were not a constant part of their daily lives and that their absence acted as a protective factor.

**Table 04. Domain: Positive Effect of the CES-D Scale presented by caregivers of the elderly in Health District IV. Recife, October/2015 to April/2016.**

| During the last week: | Rarely | For a short time | For a moderate amount of time | Most of the time |
|---|---|---|---|---|
| **08. I felt optimistic about the future** | 84 | 32 | 31 | 81 |
| **12. I've been happy** | 66 | 31 | 36 | 99 |
| **16. I've enjoyed my life** | 74 | 26 | 34 | 94 |

Table 04 shows the analysis of the positive affect domain of the scale, which shows that in item 08 I felt optimistic about the future (36.8%), there was a higher percentage of the answer rarely, showing that for this group it worked as a negative affect in relation to this variable. As for items 12 - I was happy (29%) and 16 - I enjoyed my life (32.4%), the highest percentage was for the answer "most of the time", showing that the constant presence of these items is a protective factor for the onset of depressive symptoms.

The practice of caring for the elderly, through its complications, causes the caregiver to feel various different feelings, such as exhaustion, weariness, joy, happiness and satisfaction (ANJOS et al, 2014). Caregivers can also develop positive and negative factors as a result of the great responsibility and burden of activities provided to the elderly.

However, in relation to happiness, Souza and Duarte (2013) say that being happy is a little more relevant and has a longer-lasting effect when compared to a pleasant moment of humor. When people are happy, they are less selfish, less aggressive, less offensive and less prone to illness. They are more reliable, affectionate, kind, flexible, creative, committed and always determined to help.

**Table 05. Domain: Somatic Symptoms of the CES-D Scale presented by caregivers of the elderly in Health District IV. Recife, Oct/2015 to April/2016.**

| During the last week: | Rarely | For a short time | For a moderate amount of time | Most of the time |
|---|---|---|---|---|
| 01. I felt uncomfortable | 142 | 37 | 22 | 27 |
| 02. I didn't feel like eating | 145 | 26 | 24 | 33 |
| 05. Difficulty in concentrate | 130 | 23 | 43 | 32 |
| 07. Making an effort to cope with the usual tasks | 99 | 34 | 46 | 49 |
| 11. Sleep was not restful | 105 | 23 | 34 | 66 |

Table 05 shows the analysis of the somatic symptoms domain of the scale. The answer rarely occurred in all the items (1, 2, 5, 7 and 11), which determined them as protective factors, minimizing the appearance of depressive symptoms. The variables are: I felt uncomfortable (62.2%), I didn't feel like eating (63.5%), I had trouble concentrating (57%), I struggled to do my usual tasks (43.4%), and my sleep wasn't restful (46%), respectively.

The symptoms of depression show different characteristics, such as a lack of energy and enthusiasm for life, as well as a feeling of emptiness and discouragement. Mood becomes low, with symptoms such as lack of concentration and desire to perform previously enjoyable tasks, changes in appetite and sleep, feelings of frustration and, in more complex cases, thoughts of death (SOUSA et al, 2013). Therefore, in view of the results, and making reference to the aforementioned study, the caregivers of elderly people investigated in this research have almost zero chance of developing depression, given that their responses were all positive for the variables in the somatic domain.

**Table 06. Interpersonal domain of the CES-D Scale presented by caregivers of the elderly in**

**Health District IV. Recife, October/2015 to April/2016.**

| During the last week: | Rarely | For a short time | For a moderate amount of time | Most of the time |
| --- | --- | --- | --- | --- |
| **04. I compared myself to other people in terms of value** | 169 | 26 | 14 | 19 |
| **15. People weren't friendly** | 127 | 43 | 28 | 30 |
| **19. People don't like me** | 149 | 28 | 32 | 19 |

Table 06 shows the analysis of the interpersonal domain in terms of the scale, showing that all the variables were positive in relation to the response rarely. Items 4, 15 and 19 correspond to: I compared myself to other people in terms of value (74.1%), people weren't friendly (55.7%) and people didn't like me (65.3%), respectively. As the answers were rare, it shows that not comparing oneself to others in terms of personal value, living in friendly relationships and liking oneself are factors that reduce the risk of depressive symptoms.

Thus, Ferraresi and Barham (2014) talk about the importance of social interactions, insofar as they represent a health protection factor, since, by relating to others, it is possible to build bonds and engage in a progressive degree of activity, resulting in access to social support networks, which, in turn, help to get through crises, improve self-esteem and personal success.

Pinto and Barham (2014) say that social competencies are skills that help to initiate and preserve positive and favorable relationships, which can result in satisfactory social harmony in the environment.

**Graph 01. Depressive symptoms in caregivers related to initiative for activities of daily living. - CES-D - Batistoni, Neri, Cupertino. Informant from Health District IV. Recife, October/2015 to April/2016.**

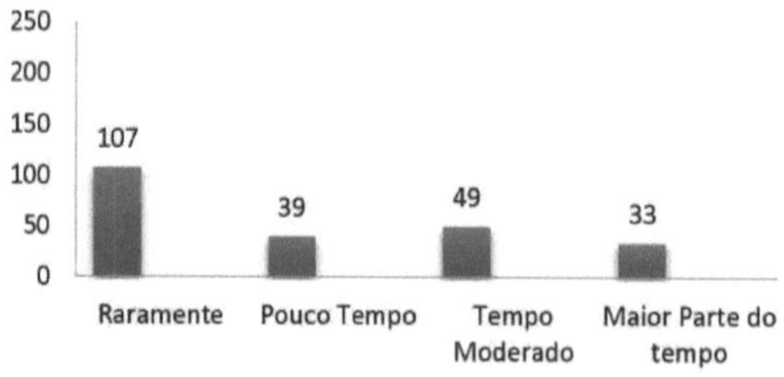

Graph 01 shows the caregivers' response to the item: "I wasn't able to get on with my life", which had a predominance of the option "rarely" by 46.9% of the elderly caregivers. This leads us to understand that if people manage to carry on with their lives despite all the difficulties related to caring, they are less exposed to depressive symptoms.

Martins and Mestre (2014) say that, nowadays, quality of life can range from personal satisfaction to social well-being. This perception is also found in a less comprehensible way, such as self-esteem, dignity, the possibility of achieving personal goals, satisfaction with life, happiness and positive thinking about oneself and the future.

## CONCLUSION

The study concluded that the analysis of the scale of depressive symptoms in caregivers of the elderly (CES-D), when used as an analysis of the domains and items that make it up, allows a broader view of the issues related to these symptoms. This can lead to a reflection on the domains of the items in isolation and provide a reading of the precipitating or protective factors of stress arising from caregiving, leading to a deeper reflection and knowledge of this issue.

Identifying the profile of these elderly caregivers provides a reflection on their sociodemographic characteristics and their responses to depressive symptoms, which can be further developed and explored in new studies.

We hope that the knowledge from this study will contribute to improving the quality of life of these caregivers and will be a useful tool for nurses who are health educators and who, in primary care, work as a form of prevention in order to provide well-being in all areas of the individual's life, in other words, in all biopsychosocial areas.

In this way, we can open up a range of possibilities for new reflections on this subject and all the wealth of details that can be explored, generating benefits for science, for carers of the elderly and for nursing, where the fundamental part of its work should not be exclusively the biological body, but also the human being in all its particularities.

## REFERENCES

AGUIAR, Elizabeth SS *et al* . Representaçoes sociais do cuidar de idosos para cuidadores: Revisao Integrativa. **rev. Sick UERJ** , 2011. v. 19, n. 3, p. 485-490.

ANJOS, Karla Ferraz dos *et al* ., (2014). Perfil de cuidadores familiares de idosos no domicilio.

**rev. fishing i care foundation** [online], 2014. v. 6, n. 2, p. 450-461.

ARAÙJO, Jefferson Santos *et al* . Perfil dos cuidadores e as difficiles enfrentadas no cuidado ao idoso, em Ananindeua, PA. **rev. Arm. Geriatrician Gerontol.** [online], 2013. v. 16, n. 1, p. 149-158. doi: < http://dx.doi.org/10.1590/S1809-98232013000100015 >.

BATISTONI, Samila Sathler Tavares; NERI, Anita Liberalesso; CUPERTINO, Ana Paula. Validade e confiabilidade da versao brasileira da Center for Epidemiological Scale - Depression (CES-D) em idosos brasileiros. **Psico - USF** , 2010. v. 15, n. 1, p. 13-22. doi: < http://dx.doi.org/10.1590/S1413-82712010000100003 >.

PHILIPPINES, Nadiesca Taisa *et al* . Quality of life of subjects with Parkinson's disease e seus cuidadores **Physiotherapist. Purple** [online], 2014. v. 27, n. 1, p. 57-66. doi: <http://dx.doi.org.10.1590/0103-5150.027.001.AO06>.

GRATÂO, Aline Cristina Martins *et al* . Sobrecarga e desconforto emocional em cuidadores de idosos. **Texto Contexto Enferm.** [online], 201. v. 19, n. 3, p. 304-12. doi: < http://dx.doi.org/10.1590/S0104-07072012000200007 >.

MARTINS, Rosa Maria Lopes; MASTERS, Marina Alexandra. Esperança e Qualidade na vida de idosos. **Millenium** [online], 2014. v. 47, p. 153-162. Available at: < http://www.ipv.pt/millenium/Millenium47/13.pdf >.

OLIVEIRA, Déborah Cristina; D'ELBOUX, Maria José. Estudos nacionais sobre cuidadores familiares de idosos: integrative review. **rev. Arm. Sick** [online], 2012. v. 65, n. 5, p. 829-38. doi: < http://dx.doi.org/10.1590/S0034-71672012000500017 >.

OLIVEIRA, Marcos Francisco *et al* . Autorreferida depressao symptomatology por idosos que vivem em comunidade. **Ciência & Saùde Coletiva** [online], 2012. v. 17, n. 8, p. 2191 2198. doi: < http://dx.doi.org/10.1590/S1413-81232012000800029 >.

PEREIRA, Roberta Amorim *et al* . Sobrecarga dos cuidadores de idosos com stroke stroke. **rev. Esc Enferm** [online], 2013. v. 47, n. 1, p. 185-92. doi: < http://dx.doi.org/10.1590/S0080-62342013000100023 >.

PINTO, Francine Nathalie Ferraresi Rodrigues; BARHAM, Elizabeth Joan. Psychological well-being : Comparaçao entre cuidadores de idosos com e sem demência. **Psicologia, health and disease** [online], 2014. v. 15, n. 3, p. 635-655. doi: < http://dx.doi.org/10.15309/14psd150307 >.

PINTO, Francine Nathalie Ferraresi Rodrigues; BARHAM, Elizabeth Joan. Social skills and stress coping strategies : relationship with indicators of psychological well-being and care for elderly people with other addictions. **rev. Arm. Geriatrician Gerontol.** [online], 2014. v. 17, n. 3, p. 525-

539. doi: < http://dx.doi.org/10.1590/1809- 9823.2014.13043 >.

SANTOS, Nilce Maria de Freitas; TAVARES, Darlene Mara dos Santos. Correlaçao entre qualidade de vida e morbidade do cuidador de idoso com accidente vascular encefàlico. **Rev Esc Enferm** [online], 2012. v. 46, n. 4, p. 960-966. two: < http://dx.doi.org/10.1590/S0080-62342012000400025 >.

SANTOS, Gerson de Souza; CUNHA, Isabel Cristina Kowal Olm. Perfil sociodemogràfico de cuidadores familiares de idosos residentes em uma area de abrangência da Estratégia Saùde da Familia no municipio de Sao Paulo. **Saùde Coletiva** [online], 2013. v. 10, n. 60, p. 47-53. Available at: < http://www.redalyc.org/pdf/842/84228212008.pdf >.

SOUSA, Ana Carla Santos Nogueira de; BOSCHETTI, Deborah Inàcio da Silva; SUZIKI, Maria Alzira Guimaraes Mendes. Human communication is depressao: Repercussions no aging. **Portai de Divulgaçâo magazine** , 2013. v. 30, Year III, p. 19-27. ISSN 2178-3454.

SOUZA, Luciana Karine de; DUARTE, Mônica Grace. Amizade is Bem-Estar subjective. **Psych: Theor. it's Pesq.** [online], 2013. v. 29, n. 4, p. 429-436. doi: <http://dx.doi .org/ 10.1590/S0102-37722013000400009>.

STACKFLETH, Renata *et al* . Sobrecarga de trabalho em cuidadores de idosos fragilizados que vivem no domicilio. **Acta Paul Enferm** [online], 2012. v. 25, n. 5, p. 768-774. doi: < http://dx.doi.org/10.1590/S0103-21002012000500019 >.

TOMOMITSU, Mônica RSV; PERRACINI, Mônica Rodrigues; NERI, Anita Liberalesso. The influence of gender, idade e renda sobre o well-estar de idosos cuidadores e nao cuidadores. **rev. Arm. Geriatrician Gerontol.** [online], 2013. v. 16, n. 4, p. 663-680. doi: < http://dx.doi.org/10.1590/S1809-98232013000400002 >.

YAMASHITA, Cintia Hotomi *et al* . Association between a social support and a profile of family caregivers of patients with disabilities and dependence. **rev. Esc. Enferm** [online], 2013. v. 47, n. 6, p. 1359-1366. doi: < http://dx.doi.org/10.1590/S0080- 623420130000600016 >.

# CHAPTER 02: PROFILE OF CARERS OF THE ELDERLY AND ANALYSIS OF THE DOMAINS OF AN OVERLOAD SCALE


[1]Gardênia Conceiçao Santos de Souza,[2] Eliana Lessa Cordeiro,[3] Liniker Scolfild Rodrigues da Silva,[4] Diana Marques Cunha,[4] Carlos Henrique da Silva Ferreira, [4]Fernanda Santos Cavalcanti,[4] Izis Santana da Silva,[4] Karla Roberta Leite de Lima, [4]Dayse Andrielle Viana da Silva,[4] Maria Jocélia Silva de Souza,[4] Luana Carla de Andrade Palha.

[1]Master's Degree in Gerontology from the Federal University of Pernambuco (UFPE). Recife

(PE), Brazil. E-mail: gardeniacss@yahoo.com.br

[2]Master's Degree in Neuropsychiatry and Behavioral Sciences from the

Federal University of

Pernambuco (UFPE). Recife (PE), Brazil. E-mail:

elianalessa18@hotmail.com

[3]Resident in the Multiprofessional Residency Program in Collective Health at the Faculty of Medical Sciences (FCM) and the University of Pernambuco (UPE).

Recife, Pernambuco (PE), Brazil. E-mail: liniker 14@hotmail.com

[4]Nurses (graduates), Salgado de Oliveira University (UNIVERSO). Recife, Pernambuco (PE), Brazil. E-mail: fernandacsantos.87@gmail.com;

izisantana@gmail.com; karlaroberta571 @gmail.com; andrielledaysev@gmail.com; joocelia@gmail.com; luanapalha@gmail.com; diana.marques.cunha@gmail.com;

carlos.henrique.sf.ch@gmail.com


## SUMMARY


**Objective: To** identify the sociodemographic profile of elderly caregivers and to evaluate their responses to the domains of a burden scale. **Method:** This is a descriptive cross-sectional study with a quantitative approach, in which the ZARIT BURDEN scale was used to analyze the domains and their items. The sample consisted of 228 forms, applied to caregivers of elderly people registered with the Family Health Program in Health District IV, with the inclusion criterion being age 28 or over and at least 10 years living with the elderly. **Results:** The study showed that the profile of caregivers of the elderly was predominantly female, aged between 50 and 60, with primary schooling, marital status married or in a stable union, and social class D-E. An analysis of the scale's domains showed that there was a prevalence of the answer "never" in the "impact on caregiving" domain. As for the interpersonal relationship domain, there was a predominance of the answer never, with the exception of the penultimate item, which was answered always. In the domain of expectations of care, the most common answer was never, with the exception of the last two items, which were always answered. The variation in responses validated all the items as protective of caregiver burden. **Conclusion:** This study has shown the importance of using the scales and analyzing the domains and their isolated items to reflect on each factor and its impact on caregiver burden and, together with knowledge of the profile of caregivers of the elderly, has led to discussions on this topic.

**Keywords:** Overload; Caregivers; Elderly.

## INTRODUCTION

A caregiver is defined as someone who is responsible for looking after the sick or dependent elderly person, facilitating their daily activities, such as feeding, personal hygiene, as well as administering routine medication and accompanying them to health services or other activities of the elderly person's daily life, excluding techniques and functions that are the preserve of nurses and doctors (NARDI et al, 2011).

There are differences between caregivers, who can be called formal or informal. The former are characterized by the provision of professional services, while the latter can be family members, friends, neighbors or others who care for the elderly in a family environment (FERREIRA, 2012).

In addition to the physical effort, the caregiver needs to be attentive to some procedures that require concentration, such as administering medication, in order to obtain satisfactory care results (SEQUEIRA, 2010).

The act of caring should be one of total self-giving, without expecting anything in return, such as recognition and affection from the elderly person to the caregiver. Caregiving can generate feelings of love, gratitude and affection as a form of recognition on the part of the elderly person for the care and attention received, making the elderly person and caregiver closer in this new relationship, but it can also generate contrary feelings on the part of the caregiver towards the elderly person, such as guilt, anger, fear and anguish, generating the situation of caregiver overload (VITALIANO et al, 2012).

The term overload is used in the literature to talk about the negativity of the task of caring for the caregiver. It is the physical and mental exhaustion of caregivers due to exposure to stress factors (SEQUEIRA et al, 2010).

Overload can be seen objectively and subjectively. Objective overload deals with the demands of caring for the elderly person's severity, dependency and behavior, and the consequences have a direct impact on the caregiver's life in various areas (family, social, economic and professional); subjective overload is linked to the caregiver's emotional state when caring for the elderly person, i.e. the extent to which this emotional state affects care and the relationship between them (GRATAO et al, 2012).

As the caregiver realizes that their family relationships are being directly impacted by this overload, the first signs and symptoms begin to develop, such as: fatigue, the use of additional medication, the caregiver's stress with other family members and friends, in addition to having their health impaired, which can impact their care for the elderly person. It also affects the social and economic areas, compromising all aspects of the caregiver's life (OLIVEIRA et al, 2015).

Oliveira & D'Elboux reviewed 76 Brazilian studies and also identified high levels of caregiver burden, with a greater burden for those in unfavorable sociodemographic conditions (LINO et al, 2016).

The problems that affect the life and health of the caregiver should be screened to enable prevention and generate instruction so that these caregivers can create ways to reconcile all the activities imposed on them, improving their quality of life, reducing the impact on their health and providing better care for the elderly (STACKFLETH et al, 2012).

With this in mind, the general aim of this article was to identify the sociodemographic profile of caregivers of the elderly in terms of age, gender, education, marital status and social class, and to analyze their responses to the *Zarit Burden* Scale and all the domains and items that make it up. To do this, it was necessary to classify the sample, list the items in the domains of the *Zarit Burden* scale and separate them into separate tables and graphs, containing the domains and their respective items.

## METHOD

This is a cross-sectional, descriptive study with a quantitative approach that aimed to identify the sociodemographic profile of caregivers of the elderly and analyze their responses to the domains of the *Zarit Burden* Scale, which made it possible to obtain, organize, analyze data and respond to the collection instrument.

The target population was made up of caregivers of elderly people registered with the Family Health Programs (PSF's) in District IV, in the city of Recife/PE, and the inclusion criteria were having known the elderly person for at least 10 years and being aged 28 or over. The high number of elderly people and their caregivers in this district was considered a criterion for choosing this population.

The sample was calculated based on the number of elderly people registered in the PSFs, using the STATCALC program, with the following parameters: population of 32,960 elderly people in Health District IV, 95% confidence interval. The number of caregivers corresponds to the number of elderly people, resulting in a total of 244 which, after losses due to collection limitations, resulted in 228 interviewees.

The data collection instrument used in the research was the *Zarit Burden* instrument, validated for Brazil by Carlos Alberto da Cruz Sequeira on January 25, 2010. This scale, in its original version, consisted of 29 questions, which included aspects related to physical and psychological health, economic resources, work, social relationships and the relationship with the "care receiver". This instrument was later revised and reduced to 22 items. Each item is scored quantitatively as follows: never = (0); rarely = (1); sometimes = (2); almost always = (3) and always = (4). The quantitative score varies from zero to four points for each item, with a cut-off point of 20 points. The Zarit Caregiver Burden Scale (ZCBS) has three domains: Impact of caregiving, interpersonal relationship and expectations of caregiving, each with its own items.

Data was collected through face-to-face interviews, using the sociodemographic questionnaire created based on the criteria of the Brazilian Association of Research Companies (ABEP) and the *Zarit Burden* scale validated for Brazil, from September 2015 to April 2016.

The data used was provided by researcher and professor Gardênia Conceiçao Santos de Souza, as part of the database for her dissertation, entitled: COGNITIVE DECLINE IN THE ELDERLY - TRACKING FROM THE ELDERLY AND THEIR INFORMANT. The other participating authors were part of the PIC (Scientific Initiation Project) at the Salgado de Oliveira University (UNIVERSO), Recife campus, where the aforementioned professor is an advisor.

The research only began after the project was approved by the Ethics and Research Committee (CEP) of the Federal University of Pernambuco (UFPE), under CAAE: 48403115.8.0000.5208, respecting the principles of privacy, reliability and fairness.

During the research, all the precepts of Resolution No. 466/12 of the National Health Council (CNS) were respected with regard to ethical aspects involving human beings, the signing of the Informed Consent Form (ICF), the risks and benefits and the responsibilities of the researcher.

The forms were applied individually and, after obtaining the data, they were compiled manually, with their items numbered to generate the domain tables according to the classification given by the author, which gave rise to tables and a graph created in the Excel 2010 program, with the values calculated in absolute and relative frequency and analyzed in the light of Brazilian and international scientific literature.

## RESULTS AND DISCUSSION

Through the sociodemographic questionnaire, the profile of elderly caregivers was verified. Table 01 shows the sociodemographic characteristics of the caregivers of elderly people in district IV, surveyed in the city of Recife between September 2015 and April 2016. It was observed that the majority of the caregivers interviewed were female 186 (81.58%), aged between 50 and 60 59 (25.88%), had elementary school education 98 (43%) and were married or in a stable union 96 (42.10%).

**Table 01. Sociodemographic characterization of elderly caregivers in Health District IV. Recife, October/2015 to April/2016.**

| Variables | n = 228 | % |
|---|---|---|
| **Sex** | | |
| Female | 186 | 81,58 |
| Male | 42 | 18,42 |
| **Age** | | |
| 28 --\| 38 | 49 | 21,5 |

| 39 --\| 49 | 47 | 20,61 |
| 50 --\| 60 | 59 | 25,88 |
| 61 --\| 71 | 53 | 23,24 |
| > 72 | 20 | 8,77 |

**Continuation of Table 01. Sociodemographic characterization of elderly caregivers in Health District IV. Recife, October/2015 to April/2016.**

| **Education** | | |
| --- | --- | --- |
| Illiterate | 25 | 11,0 |
| Fundamental | 98 | 43,0 |
| Medium | 81 | 35,5 |
| Superior | 24 | 10,5 |
| **Marital status** | | |
| Single | 95 | 41,67 |
| Married or in a stable union | 96 | 42,10 |
| Viùvo | 19 | 8,33 |
| Other | 18 | 7,90 |

The study by Stackfleth et al, (2012) showed a predominance of married female caregivers, who are generally the daughters or wives of the elderly, and cited that this characteristic is common in several studies, both nationally and internationally. These findings reinforced the social role of women, historically determined as caregivers. In addition, the study by Pereira et al, (2013), says that the fact that caregivers are married can be positive or negative, since caregivers with this marital status can have the support of their partner in caring for the elderly, but, on the other hand, they accumulate functions due to the attributions of husband or wife, father or mother.

With regard to the average age of caregivers, those aged between 50 and 60 prevailed 59 (25.88%), followed by 61 to 71 (23.24%), with a small difference between these variables.

This finding corroborates the study by Hedler et al, (2016) which observed the existence of elderly and middle-aged people caring for elderly people. From this perspective, elderly family caregivers are more subject to the negative impacts of caregiving, since they generally have the same living conditions as the elderly person they care for, and also experience the changes of aging itself. Caring for a dependent elderly person can cause caregivers to worry that they may be approaching their own dependence or finitude.

Lima and Junior (2015) said that older caregivers seem to be more susceptible to overload, but younger caregivers may suffer more isolation and greater social restrictions, proportional to the greater possibilities for social and leisure activities in their age group.

With regard to schooling, 98 (42.98%) had primary schooling, followed by 81 (35.52%) with a lower level of secondary schooling. Studies show that caregivers of the elderly have a low level of income due to their lack of schooling and show the association between fragile financial conditions and low schooling as strong indicators of stress in this population (COELHO et al, 2013).

**Table 02. Social class Brazil (ABEP, 2015) of caregivers of the elderly in Health District IV. Recife, October/2015 to April/2016.**

| Variables | Points | n = 228 | % |
| --- | --- | --- | --- |
| A | 45-100 | 04 | 02 |
| B1 | 38-44 | 10 | 4,3 |
| B2 | 29-37 | 34 | 15 |
| C1 | 23-28 | 53 | 23,2 |
| C2 | 17-22 | 55 | 24 |
| D-E | 0-16 | 72 | 31,5 |

Table 02 shows the characterization of the social class Brazil (ABEP, 2015) of the caregivers of the elderly in district IV in Recife from September to April 2016. It can be seen that the majority of caregivers belong to social class D-E 72 (31.5%). This problem has been reflected in Brazil since the 1990s, with the creation of the Real Plan. Although this is a widespread phenomenon, as other authors have pointed out, the increase in the D-E classes involves workers and other wage earners who have been most affected, as well as the lower middle class (JANNUZZI, 2013).

The study by Rondini et al, (2011), confirms this data, stating that, in relation to the social class of those involved, 28.5% belong to class A (population in good living conditions), 19.4% to class B (population in good living conditions, but with some deficits), 18.8% are from class C (population with living conditions classified as regular) and the remaining

33.3%, from class D, classified as having poor living conditions.

**Table 03. Impact on caregiving domain of the ZARIT BURDEN scale presented by caregivers of the elderly in Health District IV. Recife, October 2015 to April 2016.**

| Variables | Never | Rarely | To Times | Almost always | Always |
|---|---|---|---|---|---|
| 01. You feel you need more help | 94 | 39 | 40 | 25 | 34 |
| 02. Lacks time | 129 | 41 | 36 | 12 | 15 |
| 03. Feels stressed | 151 | 20 | 43 | 07 | 10 |
| 09. You feel tension | 184 | 12 | 21 | 09 | 04 |
| 10. You feel it affects your health | 190 | 17 | 15 | 04 | 06 |
| 11. Lacks privacy | 165 | 15 | 26 | 05 | 18 |
| 17. You feel you've lost control of your life | 179 | 09 | 25 | 03 | 13 |

In table 03, the analysis of the domain of the scale regarding the impact on caregiving showed that all the items gave the highest percentage for the answer NEVER. Caregivers say they never feel that the elderly person asks for more help than they need 94 (41.22%), never feel a lack of time 129 (56.57%), never feel stressed 151 (66.22%), never feel tense 184 (80.70%), never feel that care has affected their health 190 (83.33%), never feel a lack of privacy 165 (72.36%) and never feel that they have lost control of their lives 179 (78.50%). Therefore, with regard to this domain, in the absence of impacts related to the provision of direct care, such as the elderly person not asking for more help than they need, the caregiver not feeling a lack of time for themselves, not feeling stressed, not feeling tense, not feeling that care affects their health, not feeling a lack of privacy and not feeling that they have lost control of their life, these items alone are transformed into protective factors against overload, so that the caregiver can offer better and more effective care to the elderly person.

According to the study by Lino et al, (2016), the task of caring often leads to depression and reduced quality of life, and the main source of burden is the degree of dependence of the individual receiving care.

Rocha (2013) states that, from the perspective of a caregiver or family member, the situation of caring for an elderly person, whether dependent or not, constitutes a crisis situation, as there is a significant change in the direction of their life. In this way, formal or informal caregiving emerges as a strong stressor, which disrupts or threatens the caregiver's usual activity.

On the other hand, the study showed that, for the sample studied, these factors did not interfere with the quality of life of caregivers, causing the appearance of signs of overload, because they were not present in their daily lives, thus becoming protective factors of overload.

**Table 04. Domain: Interpersonal relationship of the ZARIT BURDEN scale presented by caregivers of the elderly in Health District IV. Recife, October/2015 to April/2016.**

| Variables | Never | Rarely | Sometimes | Almost Always | Always |
|---|---|---|---|---|---|
| **04. Feels ashamed** | 196 | 14 | 13 | 04 | 01 |
| **05. Feels irritated** | 181 | 20 | 19 | 06 | 02 |
| **06. You feel it affects your relationships** | 176 | 26 | 20 | 05 | 03 |
| **12. You feel your social life is being damaged** | 185 | 15 | 16 | 07 | 05 |
| **13. Doesn't feel comfortable receiving visitors** | 179 | 11 | 14 | 10 | 14 |
| **16. Feels able to care for longer** | 27 | 11 | 22 | 35 | 133 |
| **19. Feeling uncertain about what to do** | 154 | 14 | 30 | 10 | 20 |

In table 04, the analysis of the interpersonal relationship domain of the scale, the predominant response was NEVER for items 04. Never feel

embarrassed 196 (85.96%), 05. They never feel irritated 181 (79.38%), 06. They have never felt that caring negatively affects their relationships 176 (77.19%), 12. They have never felt that caring harms their social life 185 (81.14%), 13. They never feel uncomfortable receiving visitors 179 (78.50%) and 19- They never feel uncertain about what to do for the elderly 154 (67.54%), showing that the answer "never" for these items works as a factor in reducing the risk of overload. As for item 16, which asks how capable they feel of looking after the elderly for longer, the most prevalent answer was always 133 (58.33%), showing that the answer to this item also works as a positive factor in relation to this variable.

With regard to interpersonal relationships, when the caregiver doesn't feel ashamed or irritated, doesn't feel that care negatively affects their relationships, doesn't feel that care harms their social life, says they never feel uncomfortable receiving visitors, and never feels in doubt about what to do for the elderly person, the caregivers don't show negative signs in their interpersonal relationship with the dependent person and, consequently, don't show signs of overload.

Ferreira (2012) says that it is the family or, in particular, the caregivers who bear the greatest responsibility, who enter into situations of crisis and breakdown, manifesting tension, embarrassment, fatigue, stress, frustration, reduced socializing, depression and altered self-esteem.

**Table 05. Domain: Expectations of care on the ZARIT BURDEN scale presented by caregivers of elderly people in Health District IV. Recife, October/2015 to April/2016.**

| Variables | Never | Rarely | To Times | Almost Always | Always |
|---|---|---|---|---|---|
| **07. Fear for the future** | 95 | 26 | 52 | 17 | -- |
| **08. Feels dependent on you** | 73 | 28 | 46 | 20 | 61 |
| **14. Feels that only you can take care of him** | 104 | 18 | 31 | 18 | 57 |
| **15. Feels he has no money** | 93 | 18 | 37 | 26 | 54 |
| **18. Would like someone else to take care of you** | 165 | 19 | 19 | 13 | 12 |
| **20. Do you feel you could do more** | 47 | 11 | 35 | 35 | 99 |
| **21. Feels they could take better care** | 48 | 21 | 41 | 28 | 90 |

In table 05, the analysis of the domain of the scale regarding expectations of care showed that the majority of interviewees answered never, although a significant number answered always. The most prevalent answers were never for items 07. Never fear for the elderly person's future 95 (41.66%), 08. Never feel dependent on the elderly person 73 (32.01%), also considering the high rate of caregivers who said they always feel this dependence 61 (26.75%), 14. Never feel as if they are the only person who can look after them 104 (45.61%), 15. Never feel like they don't have enough money 93 (40.78%), 18. Never feel like someone else would take care of the elderly 165 (72.36%). Items 20 Feel they could do more for the elderly 99 (43.42%) and 21 Feel they could take better care of them 90

(39.47%) had a prevalent response of always.

Therefore, with regard to expectations of care, it was noted that the answers in this domain indicate that, for the sample studied, the answer never for the first items (07, 08, 14, 15, 18) and always for the last two (20, 21), even with different meanings, when attributed to the item in isolation, work as factors to reduce the appearance of caregiver overload.

According to Almeida et al, (2016), in their study, the caregivers' perceptions of how they feel performing the role of care showed that, although care interferes with physical and emotional health, most feel good about being able to care for their family member. Many reported a sense of gratification, pride and accomplishment at having the chance to help someone important in their lives.

Barros et al, (2011), say that there can be ambiguities when it comes to expectations about caring for the elderly. In this case, satisfaction is observed when caregivers are emotionally and economically structured. When these resources are insufficient, it can lead to tension in caregiving and, ultimately, mistreatment of the elderly.

**Graph 01. Symptoms of overload related to the impact on the provision of care among informants in Health District IV. - ZARIT BURDEN - Sequeira. Recife, October/2015 to April/2016.**

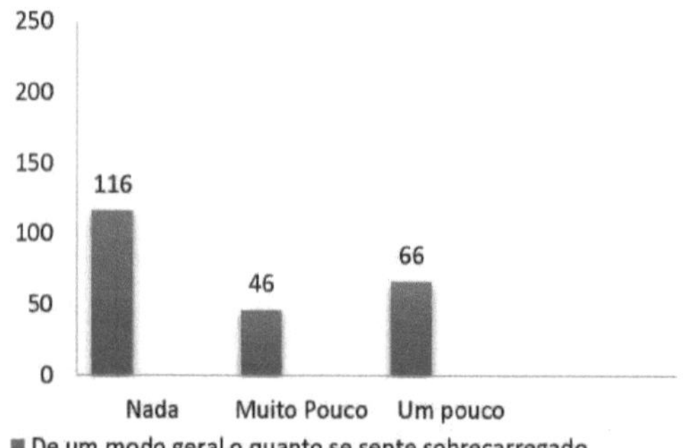


Graph 01 shows the answers to the question of whether the caregiver feels overburdened by care, the most prevalent answer being: 116 said nothing (50.87%). Not feeling overwhelmed acts as a protective factor against the appearance of caregiver overload.

This corroborates the study by Rondini et al, (2011), which states that when caregivers were asked about a possible work overload from caring for the elderly, 60 (36.6%) said not at all.

# CONCLUSION

The study showed that, with regard to the sociodemographic data of caregivers of the elderly, the prevalence is of women, with elementary education, married or in a stable union, aged between 50 and 60 and from social class D-E. Identifying the profile of these caregivers is extremely important for understanding their sociodemographic characteristics and, when correlated with the responses to signs of overload, generates reflections in a larger and different sphere, which could be further developed and addressed in new studies.

With regard to the analysis of the domains and items of the *Zarit Burden* Caregiver *Burden* Scale, most of the answers pointed to the non-existence of the items proposed in the domains addressed, making them protective factors against the development of signs of burden. Thus, this different way of analyzing the scale, making a sub-analysis of the domains and items that make it up, provides a greater perspective for viewing the issues related to the proposed symptoms. In this way, it can contribute to reflecting on the domains and items in order to gain a deeper understanding of this subject.

We hope that the information and knowledge derived from this analysis will contribute to improving the quality of life of these caregivers and will be a useful tool for nurses who are health educators. We also hope that it can be used in primary care to prevent the development of this state of exhaustion, which can lead caregivers to physical and mental illnesses, reducing their quality of life and hindering or even preventing them from caring for the elderly.

We hope that the result will motivate new reflections on the importance of care for elderly caregivers and the creation of new studies on this topic, generating contributions to science, nursing and this group.

## REFERENCES

ALMEIDA, Roberta Rodrigues de; BORGES, Camila Dellatorre; SHUHAMA, Rosana. A processo de cuidar de idosos restritos ao domicilio: percepçoes de cuidadores familiares. **His magazine. & Transfer Soc** [online], 2016. v. 7, n. 2, p. 93-105.

ANDRADE, Fernanda Maria Mendes de. **An informal cuidador a pessoa idosa dependente em contexto domiciliàrio: necesias educativas do cuidador principal.** 2009. 359 f. Dissertaçao (Mestrado) - Curso de Mestrado em Ciências da Educaçao. Braga: Universidade do Minho, Instituto de Educaçao e Psicologia.

ARAÙJO, Jefferson Santos *et al* . Perfil dos cuidadores e as difficiles enfrentadas no cuidado ao idoso, em Ananindeua, PA. **rev. Arm. Geriatrician Gerontol.** [online], 2013. v. 16, n. 1, p. 149-158. doi: < http://dx.doi.org/10.1590/S1809-98232013000100015 >.

BARROS, José Deomar de Souza *et al* . Percepçao e expectación de cuidadores no processo saùde/doença na pessoa idosa. **Saùde Magazine** [online], 2010. v. 2, n. 4, p. 29-36.

COELHO, Elaine Rodrigues *et al* . Perfil sociodemogràfico e necessitas de educaçao em saùde entre cuidadores de idosos em uma unidade de saùde da familia em Ilhéus, Bahia, Brasil. **Bras magazine. Med. Fam Comunidade** [online], 2013. v. 8, n. 28, p. 172-179. doi: < http://dx.doi.org/10.5712/rbmfc8(28)496 >.

CHAIMOWICZ, Flàvio. Saùde dos idosos brasileiros as vésperas do século XXI. **Revista Saùde Pùblica** [online], 1997. v. 31, n. 2, p. 184-200. doi: < http://dx.doi.org/10.1590/S0034-89101997000200014 >.

FERREIRA, Fatima. *et al* . Validaçao da escala de Zarit: overburden do cuidador em cuidados palatitivos domiciliàrios, para populaçao portuguesa. **Cadernos de saùde** [online], 2010. v. 3, n. 2, p. 13-19. Available to:

<http://hdl.handle.net/10400.14/10936> .

GAIOLI, Cheila Cristina Leonardo de Oliveira et al. Profile of elderly people with Alzheimer's disease associated with resilience. **Texto Contexto Enferm** [online], 2012. v. 1, n. 21, p. 150-157. doi: < http://dx.doi.org/10.1590/S0104-07072012000100017 >.

GRATÂO, Aline Cristina Martins *et al* . Sobrecarga e desconforto emocional em cuidadores de idosos. **Texto Contexto Enferm.** [online], 201. v. 19, n. 3, p. 304-312. doi: < http://dx.doi.org/10.1590/S0104-07072012000200007 >.

JANNUZZI, Paulo de Martino. Mobilidade social no contexto de adversidades crescentes do mercado de trabalho brasileiro dos anos 1990. **Revista Economia e Sociedade** , 2002. v. 11, n. 2, p. 255-278.

LINO, Valéria Teresa Saraiva *et al* . Prevalência de overburden e respective factors associados em cuidadores de idosos dependententes, em uma regiao pobre do Rio de Janeiro, Brasil. **Caderno Saùde Pùblica** [online], 2016. v. 6, n. 32, p. 1-14. doi: < http://dx.doi.org/10.1590/0102-311X00060115 >.

MANOEL, Maria Fernanda, et al. As relaçoes familiares is a level of overload do cuidador familiar. **Esc. Anna Nery** [online], 2016. v. 2, n. 17, p. 346-353. doi: < http://dx.doi.org/10.1590/S1414-

81452013000200020 >.

NARDI, Tatiana de *et al* . Sobrecarga e percepçao de qualidade de vida em cuidadores de idosos do núcleo de atendimento à terceira idade do army (natiex). **Magazine. Arm.**

**Geriatrician Gerontol** [online], 2011. v. 3, n. 14, p. 511-519. doi: < http://dx.doi.org/10.1590/S1809-98232011000300011 >.

OLIVEIRA, Ana Railka de Souza *et al* . Escalas para avaliaçao de superchargea de cuidadores de pacientes com acidente vascular encephalico. Bras **magazine . Enferm** [online], 2012. v. 65, n. 5, p. 839-843. doi: < http://dx.doi.org/10.1590/S0034- 71672012000500018 >.

OLIVEIRA, Déborah Cristina de *et al* . Quality of life and burden of work in elderly care workers in outpatient care. **Texto contexto enferm** [online], 2011. v. 2, n. 20, p. 234-240. doi: < http://dx.doi.org/10.1590/S0104-07072011000200003 >.

PEREIRA, Roberta Amorim *et al* . Sobrecarga dos cuidadores de idosos com stroke stroke. **rev. Esc Enferm** [online], 2013. v. 47, n. 1, p. 185-192. doi: < http://dx.doi.org/10.1590/S0080-62342013000100023 >.

ROCHA, Bruno Miguel Parrinha. Idoso em situaçao de dependence: stress e *coping* do cuidador informal. **Acta Paul. Sick** [online], 2013. v. 26, n. 1, p. 50-56. doi: <http://dx.doi .org/10.1590/S0103-21002013000100009>.

RONDINI, Carina Alexandra *et al* . Analysis of relationships between the quality of life and the burden of care for elderly people in Assis, SP. **I'm studying. fishing Psychol.** [online], 2011. v. 11, n. 3, p. 796-820. Available to:

< http://www.revispsi.uerj.br/v11n3/artigos/pdf/v11n3a05.pdf >.

SANTOS, Dina Isabel Francisco Alberto. **As vivencias do informal cuidador na prestaçao de cuidados ao idoso dependente - Um estudo no Conselho da Lourinha** .

2014. 309 f. Dissertaçao (Mestrado) - Curso de Mestrado em Comunicaçao em Saùde, Universidade Aberta. Available at: <http://hdl.handle.net/10400.2/732 > .

SEQUEIRA, Carlos Alberto da Cruz. Adaptaçao e validationa da escala de superchargena do cuidador de Zarit. **Enferm magazine** [online], 2010. s. II, n. 12, p. 9-16. Available at: < http://www.index-f.com/referencia/2010pdf/12-0916.pdf >.

SILVA, Maria Jûlia Paes yes. Comunicaçao tem remedio: A comunicaçao nas relaçoes interpessoais em saùde. 2011. Editora Interciência, 8th [Ed] , Unit VII. pp. 349-357.

STACKFLETH, Renata *et al.* Sobrecarga de trabalho em cuidadores de idosos fragilizados que vivem no domicilio. **Acta Paul Enferm** [online], 2012. v. 25, n. 5, p. 768-774. doi: < http://dx.doi.org/10.1590/S0103-21002012000500019 >.

UESUGUI, Helena Meika *et al* . Perfil e grau de dependence de idosos e superbarca de seus cuidadores. **Acta Paul Enferm** [online], 2011. v. 5, n. 4, p. 689-94. doi: < http://dx.doi.org/10.1590/S0103-21002011000500015 >.

# CHAPTER 03: SOCIODEMOGRAPHIC PROFILE OF THE ELDERLY IN A HEALTH DISTRICT


[1]Gardênia Conceiçao Santos de Souza,[2] Eliana Lessa Cordeiro,[3] Liniker Scolfild Rodrigues da Silva,[4] Dayse Andrielle Viana da Silva,[4] Maria Jocélia Silva de Souza, [4]Luana Carla de Andrade Palha[4] Fernanda Santos Cavalcanti,[4] Izis Santana da Silva, [4]Karla Roberta Leite de Lima,[4] Diana Marques Cunha,[4] Carlos Henrique da Silva Ferreira.

[1]Master's Degree in Gerontology from the Federal University of Pernambuco (UFPE). Recife

(PE), Brazil. E-mail: gardeniacss@yahoo.com.br

[2]Master's degree in Neuropsychiatry and Behavioral Sciences from the

Federal University of

Pernambuco (UFPE). Recife (PE), Brazil. E-mail:

elianalessa18@hotmail.com

[3]Resident in the Multiprofessional Residency Program in Collective Health at the Faculty of Medical Sciences (FCM) and the University of Pernambuco (UPE).

Recife, Pernambuco (PE), Brazil. E-mail: liniker 14@,hotmail.com
[4]Nurses (graduates), Salgado de Oliveira University (UNIVERSO). Recife,

Pernambuco (PE), Brazil. E-mail: andrielledaysev@gmail.com;

joocelia@gmail.com; luanapalha@gmail.com; diana.marques.cunha@gmail.com;

carlos.henrique.sf ch@gmail.com; fernandacsantos.87@gmail.com;

izisantana@,gmail.com; karlaroberta571 @gmail.com


## SUMMARY


**Objective: To** identify the sociodemographic profile of the elderly registered at the Basic Health Units (UBS's). **Method:** This was a cross-sectional study with a quantitative approach, using a structured form to identify the profile of 229 elderly people aged 60 or over, registered with the Family Health Program (PSF). **Results:** The study showed that, in the sample surveyed, the profile found was of women (77.7%), aged between 71 and 80, brown (53.1%), with elementary school education (51.8%), widows (39.5%) and belonging to social class D-E (41.05%). **Conclusion:** The study revealed the need to identify the profile of the elderly in order to gain a better understanding of their sociodemographic characteristics, which are so important for targeting adequate care towards the needs of this population and generating more effective actions.

**Keywords:** Sociodemographic profile; Elderly; Gerontology.

## INTRODUCTION

The ageing process has been taking place in various countries, albeit at different times and rates (KANSO, 2013). This is a process that can be approached in various contexts: social, economic, intellectual and psychological, leading to a series of organic changes and various forms of ageing. The increase in longevity creates a number of challenges for Brazil that need to be overcome in order to provide quality health care for this population (LIMA et al, 2012).

The increase in the rate of ageing is growing and is taking place in the midst of numerous difficulties in expanding the health system, which leaves the elderly vulnerable to the social conditions of developing countries. The social context can generate inequalities and place the elderly in a situation of fragility, which interferes with their well-being, impacts their functional independence and their quality of life (ANDRADE et al, 2013).

The increase in the life expectancy of the elderly population is directly related to advances in medicine and improved quality of life (VOGT et al, 2012).

The factors contributing to increased longevity are improvements in environmental, educational, cultural and social conditions. It is clear that Brazilian social and economic circumstances determine unequal living and working conditions, influencing lifestyles and generating inequalities and social exclusion for the less advantaged elderly (LIMA et al, 2012).

The country's social, economic and epidemiological profile has undergone changes, generating new health demands, especially for the care of the elderly population and bringing the need for new studies on environmental, psychosocial, cultural and economic problems that can expose the living conditions of this population (FALLER; MARCON, 2013).

The lower performance of health services, coupled with more unfavorable living conditions, influences the occurrence of health problems and increases risk factors. It is worth noting that the majority of illnesses in this population are chronic, i.e. generated by an entire process of becoming ill, leading to the need for costly interventions and complex technologies (LIMA et al, 2012).

This ageing depends on political and socio-economic transformations (PORCIÙNCULA et al, 2014). Therefore, it is believed that socio-demographic data interferes with the functional capacity of the elderly and knowing this makes it possible to create ways of preventing and caring for this population with the aim of getting these elderly into active ageing and providing quality of life (LENARDT; CARNEIRO, 2013).

The aim of this study is to identify the sociodemographic profile of the elderly registered at the Basic Health Units (UBS's) in Health District IV, classifying the sample in terms of sociodemographic data, such as: gender, age, skin color, schooling, marital status and social classification.

This study aims to provide information on the socio-demographic conditions experienced by this population, which could lead to comparative studies between this and other regions of our country, encourage reflection on the health care offered and provide tools to help managers and primary health care professionals plan their health care, especially nurses, as they are the main professionals responsible for caring for the elderly and monitoring the elderly's booklet.

## METHOD

This is a descriptive, exploratory, cross-sectional study with a quantitative approach, carried out in Health District IV of the municipality of Recife, capital of the state of Pernambuco. Located in the center-east of the Northeast region, it covers an area of 218 km$^2$ and, according to the 2010 Census, had a total population of 1,537,704 in that year, of which 9.4% were elderly.

Decree 14.452 of 1988 divided the city of Recife into 94 neighborhoods, which, when grouped together, led to the need to create six Political-Administrative Regions (RPAs), each with a Health District (DS). District IV was chosen because it has the second largest elderly population, 32,960 (BRASIL, 2014).

The study population consisted of elderly people enrolled in the Family Health Strategy (ESF) of Distrito Sanitàrio IV. We opted to carry out a sample survey using a two-stage random stratification procedure, with the Health District being the first-stage unit and the Family Health Units (USFs) the second stage for applying the forms.

The sample size was calculated using the STATCALC program, using the following parameters: population of 32,960 elderly people in Health District IV, 95% confidence interval. The result was a sample of 244, which, after losses due to collection limitations, had 229 forms.

The inclusion criteria were elderly people aged over 60; registered at the USFs; who agreed to take part in the study and signed the Informed Consent Form (ICF). Exclusion criteria were: elderly people with severe cognitive impairment that made it impossible for them to respond to interviews or loss of hearing, sight and speech impairment that made it impossible for them to communicate.

The instrument used for data collection was created using the theoretical framework of the Brazilian Association of Research Companies (ABEP) under the methodology of the Brazil Economic Classification Criterion that came into force at the beginning of 2015, described in the book *Socioeconomic Stratification and Consumption in Brazil* by professors Wagner Kamakura (Rice University) and José Afonso Mazzon (FEA/USP), based on the Family Budget Survey (POF) of the Brazilian Institute of Geography and Statistics (IBGE).

The data was collected through face-to-face interviews and the forms were applied to the elderly at home between September and April 2016. 10% of the sample was carried out through a pilot study, which was reincorporated into the final study because no changes were needed to its structure. This study is part of the dissertation research of master's student Gardénia Conceiçao Santos de Souza, entitled: COGNITIVE DECLINE IN THE ELDERLY - TRACKING FROM THE ELDERLY AND THEIR INFORMANT, and also as part of the Scientific Initiation Project (PIC) of the Salgado de Oliveira University (UNIVERSO), Recife/PE campus.

The research only began after the project was approved by the Ethics and Research Committee (CEP) of the Federal University of Pernambuco (UFPE), under CAAE: 48403115.8.0000.5208, respecting the principles of privacy, reliability and fairness.

During the research, all the precepts contained in Resolution No. 466/12 of the National Health Council (CNS) regarding ethical aspects involving human beings, the ICF process, risks and benefits and the researcher's responsibilities were respected.

The data is presented in the form of tables in the Excel 2010 program. The final presentation and analysis of the data was compiled manually and the results calculated in absolute and relative frequencies. The data for social classification was compiled, calculated and analyzed in the light of the chosen literature.

## RESULTS AND DISCUSSION

In this chapter, the sociodemographic profile of the sample studied in terms of gender, age, skin color, level of education, marital status and social classification will be presented and analyzed in the light of the literature.

**Table 01. Distribution of the elderly according to sociodemographic characteristics - USF of Health District IV, Recife/PE - September/2015 to April/2016.**

| Variables | n = 229 | % |
|---|---|---|
| **Sex** | | |
| Female | 178 | 77,7 |
| Male | 51 | 22,3 |
| **Age** | | |
| 60--\|70 | 85 | 37,3 |
| 71--\|80 | 91 | 39,9 |
| 81--\|90 | 39 | 17,1 |
| 91--\|100 | 13 | 5,7 |
| > 100 | 00 | 0,0 |

**Continuation of Table 01. Distribution of the elderly according to sociodemographic characteristics - USF of Health District IV, Recife/PE - September/2015 to April/2016.**

| Variables | n = 229 | % |
|---|---|---|
| **Skin color** | | |
| White | 61 | 26,7 |
| Brown | 121 | 53,1 |
| Black | 39 | 17,1 |

| | | |
|---|---|---|
| Indigenous | 07 | 3,1 |
| **Education** | | |
| Letrado | 89 | 39 |
| Fundamental | 118 | 51,8 |
| Medium | 20 | 8,8 |
| Superior | 01 | 0,4 |
| **Marital status** | | |
| Single | 42 | 18,4 |
| Married or in a stable union | 85 | 37,7 |
| Viùvo | 90 | 39,5 |
| Others | 11 | 4,8 |

Table 1 shows the sociodemographic characterization of the elderly in District IV, carried out in Recife between September 2015 and April 2016. Among the sociodemographic variables, gender is predominantly female, accounting for 178 (77.7%) of the elderly. In reference to this data, Santos *et al,* (2013), argue that life expectancy at birth between women and men has a difference of 7.5 years more for women. This female longevity can be explained by various factors, mainly in the sphere of social life, which have changed over time. Reinforcing this justification, Barbosa *et al,* (2013), in their study in the municipality of Teresina-PI, obtained the result of 221 (61.5%) females and 138 (38.5%) males, thus stating that this data reflects the phenomenon of feminization, translated by the worldwide existence of a higher proportion of elderly women than men, when considering the total population of each sex.

In terms of age, the 71-80 age group predominated with 91 (39.9%). Santos et al, (2013), reported a predominance of subjects in the 70-80 age group, confirming the findings of the last census of the Brazilian Institute of Geography and Statistics (IBGE) in 2010.

As for skin color, the prevalence was brown 121 (53.1%). Corrêa et al, (2012), claim that, in northeastern Brazil, the brown ethnic group predominates over other colors, due to the country's strong miscegenation. Strengthening this idea, Santos (2010) justifies that the number of elderly people of brown race exceeds those of white race in the northeast of Brazil, due to the greater centralization of Afro-descendants in this region, related to the

# TIME AND WE

This book is for our own time. The book is about the time which we feel. After reading the book no one will waste time. Time is made up by thinking and that helps us. The reader must read the book carefully to find the difference between the physical time and thinking time. I have read books on real time and I mention it as physical time, but the actual time is that which we think about. I am thankful to the publisher who published my paper on time and we. Now I decide to publish a book on it because the actual time is not that which we see. The time is essential for artificial intelligence because the person or the machine which can think faster than the given time is more intelligent than other. So this book is helpful for AI also. I am thankful to my father Sri Basudeb Jana and mother Late Mira Jana for their support and effort for coming out from my bad days. I am proud of my father, mother and brother.

I am Sri Prasenjit Jana from West Bengal, India. I am a researcher of mathematics and other subjects. I published 17 research papers in international journals and authored a book named "Computer can act with language differently" in Lambert Academic Publishing. All my research papers are with a philosophical view. So this is my second book.

history of distribution of these individuals during the slavery period.

With regard to schooling, there was a predominance of elderly people with primary schooling 118 (51.8%). Santos et al, (2013), report that the result of the low level of schooling attests to the Brazilian reality, since the average number of years of study in Brazil is still excessively low, especially in the elderly population. Silva (2011), in a study carried out in the municipality of Porto Alegre - RS, found that 72 (40%) of the elderly had only attended elementary school, reinforcing the data from our study.

With regard to marital status, 90 (39.5%) elderly people are widowed, making up the highest percentage. In contrast, Fhon et al, (2013), in their study in Sao Paulo, state that the number of widowers is 75 (33.1%), thus representing the second highest percentage, second only to the group of married elderly, represented in greater numbers, corroborating our findings. This refutes our data and points to the need to study the profile of the elderly in various regions, as disparities can be found that lead to different ways of planning care for the elderly.

**Table 02. Social Class Brazil (ABEP, 2015) of the elderly in Health District IV, Recife/PE, September/2015 to April/2016.**

| Variables | Points | n = 229 | % |
| --- | --- | --- | --- |
| A | 45-100 | 04 | 1,7 |
| B1 | 38-44 | 09 | 3,9 |
| B2 | 29-37 | 34 | 14,8 |
| C1 | 23-28 | 43 | 18,8 |
| C2 | 17-22 | 45 | 19,6 |
| D-E | 0-16 | 94 | 41,05 |

Table 02 shows the characterization of the social class Brazil (ABEP, 2015) of the elderly in district IV in Recife/PE from September 2015 to April 2016. The predominant class in the elderly population was D-E, totaling 94 (41.05%) elderly people. According to Scortegagna (2012), the social situation of old age is marked by a culture that incapacitates the elderly, in which people who reach the age of 60 become incapable subjects, especially if they come from a more disadvantaged social class. Thus, the elderly end up enduring the worst conditions imposed by society: "being poor and old, in a society that only glorifies those who have possessions and esteems those who are young enough to produce and consume according to the interests of those who own the means of production" (SCORTEGAGNA, 2012 apud JORDÀO NETTO, 1997).

Data on the social class of the elderly is scarce and, through this research, it was possible to analyze that there are many elderly people from the lower classes. For this reason, Tonon (2010) advocates a strategic policy to combat poverty and for the constitution of citizenship for the underprivileged classes.

## CONCLUSION

The study showed that, in the sample surveyed, the profile found was of women aged between 71 and 80, brown, with primary schooling, widowed and belonging to social class D-E.

Identifying the profile of the elderly is necessary and of the utmost importance in order to get to know our country's elderly population in all its heterogeneity and to think about inclusive care that minimizes social differences and reduces the gap between the various ways of assisting people in their ageing process.

When comparing this study with others carried out in Brazil, we found congruences in sociodemographic characteristics such as: in Teresina, a predominance of elderly women, brown skin color for the entire northeast region and elementary school education in Porto Alegre. This comparison between Brazilian studies shows that, despite regional differences, the situation of the elderly is similar in our country, pointing to the need for an egalitarian policy to improve the quality of life of the elderly in our country.

May this study motivate new studies to add to the profile of the elderly in various regions of this country with so many socio-economic and cultural disparities and, in a greater expectation, may it generate comparative studies and foster discussions on how to work with the needs of this population, including all health professionals, especially nurses, who work in primary care with a number of elderly people who, most of the time, find themselves in unfavorable conditions.

That knowledge of the profile of the elderly is a guideline for creating actions and strategies to improve the quality of care for the elderly population.

# REFERENCES

, Luana Machado *et al*. Politicas públicas para pessoas idosas no Brasil: uma revisao integrativa. **Ciência e Saùde Coletiva** , 2013. v. 12, n. 18, p. 3543-3552. doi: < http://dx.doi.org/10.1590/S1413-812320130001200011 >.

BARBOSA, Amanda Marreiro *et al* . Dietary intake of calcium and vitamin D is associated with a level of escolaridade na pessoa idosa. **DEMETRA: Alimentaçâo, Nutriçâo e Saùde** , 2013. v. 8, n. 2, p. 173-181. doi: < http://doi.org/10.12957/demetra.2013.4082 >.

Brazilian Institute of Geography and Statistics. **I Sintese de Indicadores Sociais:** Uma Anàlise das Condiçoes de Vida da Populaçao Brasileira. 34. ed. Brasilia: Ministério do Planejamento, Orçamento e Gestao, 2014.

CORRÊA, Rita da Graça Carvalhal Frazao *et al* . Aspectos epidemiologicos, clinicos e operanais de portatores de leprosy atendidos em um serviço de referencia no estado do Maranhao. **Magazine Soc. Bra. Med. Trope.** , 2012. v. 45, n. 1, p. 89-94. doi: < http://dx.doi.org/10.1590/S0037-86822012000100017 >.

FALLER, Jossiana Wilke; MARCON, Sonia Silva. Praticas socioculturais e de cuidados à saùde de idosos em diferentes etnias. **Escola Anna Nery** , 2013. v. 17, n. 3, p. 512-519. doi: < http://dx.doi.org/10.1590/S1414-81452013000300015 >.

FHON, Jack Roberto Silva *et al* . Prevalência de quedas de idosos em situaços de fragilidade. **Revista Saùde Pùblica** , 2013. v. 4, n. 2, p. 266-73. doi: < http://dx.doi.org/10.1590/S0034-8910.2013047003468 >.

KANSO, S. Population aging process - a global panorama. **VI Workshop on Ergonomic Analysis of Work; III Encontro Mineiro de Estudos em Ergonomia; VIII Simpósio do Programa Tutorial em Domestic Economia** . Belo Horizonte, 2013. Available at: < http://www.ded.ufv.br/workshop/docs/anais/2013/Solange%20Kanso.pdf >.

LENARDT, Maria Helena; CARNEIRO, Nathalia Hammerschmidt Kolb. Associaçao entre as caracteristicas sociodemográficas ea capacidad funcional de idosos longevos da comunidade. **Cogitare Enferm** , 2013. v. 18, n. 1, p. 13-20. doi: <http://dx.doi.org/10.5380/ce.v18i1.31299> .

LIMA, Odinélia Batista Arantes *et al* . O idoso frente ao processo de égénagement: produçao cientifica em periodicos online no ambito da saùde. **15° Congresso Brasileiro dos Conselhos de Enfermagem (CBCENF)** , 2013. 8 f. Available at: < http://apps.cofen.gov.br/cbcenf/sistemainscricoes/arquivosTrabalhos/I41303.E10.T7193. D6AP.pdf >.

SANTOS, Iraqi dos; GUERRA, Renata Gomes; SILVA, Leandro Andrade yes. Individual characteristics and clinics of elderly people with diabetes: thematic investigation in the sociopoética office. **Enferm magazine. UERJ** , 2013. v. 21, n. 1, p. 34-40. doi: <https://doi.org/10.12957/reuerj.2013.6344> .

SANTOS, Gerson de Souza. **Qualidade de vida de idosos residents em uma area de abrangência da strategy saùde da familia do municipio de Guarulhos - SP.** 2010. 96 f. Dissertaçao (Mestrado) - Curso de Mestrado em Enfermagem, Universidade de Guarulhos, Guarulhos, 2010. Available at: < http://tede.ung.br/bitstream/123456789/241/1/Gerson+de+Souza+Santos.pdf >.

SILVA, Diego Augusto Santos. Perfil sociodemogràfico e antropometrico de idosos de grupos de convivência. **I'm studying. forbidden Envelhec** , 2011. v. 16, n. 1, p. 23-39.

SCORTEGAGNA, Paola Andressa; OLIVEIRA, Rita de Càssia da Silva. Elderly: a new social actor. **IX ANPED SUL - Seminàrio de Pesquisa em Educação da Regiao Sul** , 2012. 17 f. Available at:

< http://www.ucs.br/etc/conferencias/index.php/anpedsul/9anpedsul/paper/viewFile/1886/7 3 >.

TONON, Alicia Santolini; OLIVEIRA, Dayane Aparecida Lacerda; BUSSULA, Danila Aparecida. The elderly care policy. **III Encontro de Iniciaçao Cientifica e II Encontro de Extensao Universitària** , 2007. v. 3, n. 3, p. 1-14.

VOGT, Rudiar Anderson Dorr; OLIVEIRA, Aline Sampaio of; NOLL, Matias. Estudos sobre idosos no meio acadêmico. **rev. Digital EF Desportes, Buenos Aires** , 2012. v. 16, n. 165.

# ABOUT THE AUTHORS

**Author: Gardénia Conceiçâo Santos de Souza**

Master's in Gerontology from the Department of Social Medicine - Academic Level at the Federal University of Pernambuco (UFPE) (2016); Master's in Education from the Lusophone University of Humanities and Technologies (2012); Specialist in Occupational Nursing from the Brazilian Institute of Postgraduate Studies and Extension (IBPEX) (2009). Graduated in Nursing (Bachelor) and Obstetrics from UFPE; Degree in Nursing from UFPE (2012). She is currently a lecturer at

Salgado de Oliveira University (UNIVERSO), Recife campus; Lecturer at Escada College (FAESC); Coordinator of the Nursing Residency Preparation Program at Espaço Héber Vieira. She has experience in the field of Nursing, with an emphasis on Nursing in Elderly Health and Public Health, working mainly on the following subjects: Family Health Program, aging and the elderly. Other areas of expertise are: Nursing in Communicable Diseases and Workers' Health and Adult Health.

# ABOUT THE AUTHORS

**Contributing author: Eliana Lessa Cordeiro**

Master's Degree in Neurosciences from the Postgraduate Program in Neuropsychiatry and Behavioral Science (Posneuro) - Academic Level at the Federal University of Pernambuco (UFPE) (2017); Master's Degree in Nursing from the Department of Nursing - Professional Level at the Alagoas State University of Health Sciences (UNCISAL) (2009); Specialist in Preceptorship in the SUS at the Sirio Libanês Institute (ISL) (2017); Specialization in Professional Education in the

Health Area:

Nursing by the Oswaldo Cruz Foundation (FIOCRUZ) (2004); Sanitarian - Specialist in Public Health by the University of Ribeirao Preto (UNAERP) (2004); Specialist in Psychiatry Residency by the University of Pernambuco (UPE), at the Ulysses Pernambucano Hospital (HUP), with a scholarship from the Pernambuco State Health Department (SES/PE) (2003). She has a degree in Nursing from UFPE (2001) and a full degree in Nursing from UFPE (2003). She is currently Manager and Lecturer in the Nursing Department of the Undergraduate Nursing Course and Manager of the Lato Sensu Postgraduate Course in Public Health at the Salgado de Oliveira University (UNIVERSO), Recife campus; Tutor of the Multiprofessional Residency of the Psychosocial Care Network (RAPS) of the Recife City Hall (PCR) and a registered nurse at the Psychosocial Care Center (CAPS) - José Carlos Souto of the PCR. Journal reviewer for Revista de Trabalhos Acadêmicos; and Revista Saùde e Sociedade (Online).

## ABOUT THE AUTHORS

**Contributing author: Liniker Scolfild Rodrigues da Silva**

Resident in the Multiprofessional Residency Program in Collective Health at the University of Pernambuco (UPE) and the Faculty of Medical Sciences (FCM), with a scholarship from the Pernambuco State Health Department (SES/PE); Obstetric Nurse; Specialist in Obstetric Nursing in the Residency modality at UPE and the Nossa Senhora das Graças Nursing Faculty (FENSG), assigned to the Agamenon Magalhaes Hospital (HAM) and with a scholarship from SES/PE (2017); Sanitary -

Specialization in Public Health with an emphasis on Family Health from the INESP Faculty (National Institute of Education and Research) (2016); Contributing member of the De Repente 60 Blog (Gerontology Blog); Graduated in Nursing (Bachelor's Degree) from the Salgado de Oliveira University (UNIVERSO), Recife campus (2014). She is currently a lecturer on the lato sensu postgraduate course in Obstetric Nursing at the Faculdade Brasileira de Ensino, Pesquisa e Extensao (FABEX) in partnership with the Consultoria Brasileira de Ensino, Pesquisa e Extensao (CBPEX); Lecturer on the lato sensu post-graduate course in Obstetrics and Neonatology at INESP

(National Institute of Teaching and Research) in partnership with AGE Consultoria; Lecturer/Instructor at the Pernambuco State School of Public Health (ESPPE) on the Technical Course in Health Surveillance (CTVS). Journal reviewer for the journal Drug and Alcohol Dependence and the journal Avances en Enfermaria. He worked as a trainee with the SES/PE, carrying out activities in Epidemiological Surveillance in Hospital Settings (VEAH) at IMIP - Instituto de Medicina Integral Prof. Fernando Figueira (2014). Former volunteer at the UNIVERSO Extension Project Anjos da Enfermagem: educaçao em saúde através do lùdico, in the period 2012-2013, working at the Pernambuco Center. This project is characterized as a voluntary non-profit project supported by the COFEN/COREN-PE system, carried out at the Oswaldo Cruz University Hospital (HUOC) and is considered to be the Largest Social Responsibility Project in Brazilian Nursing.

# I want morebooks!

Buy your books fast and straightforward online - at one of world's fastest growing online book stores! Environmentally sound due to Print-on-Demand technologies.

Buy your books online at
**www.morebooks.shop**

Kaufen Sie Ihre Bücher schnell und unkompliziert online – auf einer der am schnellsten wachsenden Buchhandelsplattformen weltweit! Dank Print-On-Demand umwelt- und ressourcenschonend produziert.

Bücher schneller online kaufen
**www.morebooks.shop**